A Child's Garden of Verses Copywork Book

Compiled by: Sheri Graham

Published in the United States of America by:
Graham Family Ministries
P. O. Box 826
Moundridge, KS 67107
Our Website: www.SheriGraham.com
Email: sheri@SheriGraham.com

Introduction

Welcome to <u>A Child's Garden of Verses Copywork Book</u>. This book includes a selection of poems from the classic book, A Child's Garden of Verses. The poems are divided up into short copywork selections, to allow younger children smaller portions to copy each day. Older children can work through at a quicker pace, copying more than one section each day. There are over 70 selections – enough copywork for about three months!

However you choose to use this copywork book, we pray it will be a blessing to you and your children. Cute black and white graphics are included, which can be colored by your children to add to the beauty of the pages.

Happy copywork,

Sheri Graham
Graham Family Ministries

Poem selections taken from the following book that is in the public domain:
A CHILD'S GARDEN of VERSES
By
ROBERT LOUIS STEVENSON
ILLUSTRATED BY
MYRTLE SHELDON
M. A. DONOHUE & CO.
CHICAGO
Copyright 1916 By
M. A. DONOHUE
AND
COMPANY

BED IN SUMMER 09/25/2017

In winter I get up at night,
And dress by yellow candle light.
In summer quite the other way,
I have to go to bed by day.

IN In winter I get up at night

I have to go to bed and see
The birds still hopping on the tree,
Or hear the grown-up people's feet,
Still going past me in the street.

And does it not seem hard to you,
When all the sky is clear and blue,
And I should like so much to play,
To have to go to bed by day?

_____

. . . .

_____

_____

. . . .

_____

_____

. . . .

_____

_____

. . . .

_____

YOUNG NIGHT THOUGHT

All night long and every night,
When my mamma puts out the light
I see the people marching by,
As plain as day, before my eye.

_____
....
_____
_____
....
_____
_____
....
_____
_____
....
_____

Armies and emperors and kings,
All carrying different kinds of things,
And marching in so grand a way,
You never saw the like by day.

_____
....
_____
_____
....
_____
_____
....
_____
_____
....
_____

So fine a show was never seen
At the great circus on the green;
For every kind beast and man
Is marching in that caravan.

At first they move a little slow,
But still the faster on they go,
And still beside them close I keep
Until we reach the Town of Sleep.

PIRATE STORY

Three of us afloat in the meadow by the swing.
    Three of us aboard in the basket on the lea.
Winds are in the air, they are blowing in the spring,
And waves are on the meadow like the waves there are
      at sea.

Three of us afloat in the meadow by the swing.

Where shall we adventure, to-day that we're afloat,
    Wary of the weather and steering by a star?
Shall it be to Africa, a-steering of the boat,
    To Providence, or Babylon, or off to Malabar?

Hi! but here's a squadron a-rowing on the sea—
    Cattle on the meadow a-charging with a roar!
Quick, and we'll escape them, they're as mad as they
      can be,
The wicket is the harbor and the garden is the shore.

FAREWELL TO THE FARM

The coach is at the door at last;
The eager children, mounting fast
And kissing hands, in chorus sing:
Good-bye, good-bye, to everything!

To house and garden, field and lawn,
The meadow-gates we swung upon,
To pump and stable, tree and swing,
Good-bye, good-bye, to everything!

And fare you well for evermore,
O ladder at the hayloft door,
O hayloft where the cobwebs cling,
Good-bye, good-bye, to everything!

Crack goes the whip, and off we go;
The trees and houses smaller grow;
Last, round the woody turn we swing:
Good-bye, good-bye, to everything!

THE LAND OF COUNTERPANE

When I was sick and lay a-bed,
I had two pillows at my head,
And all my toys beside me lay
To keep me happy all the day.

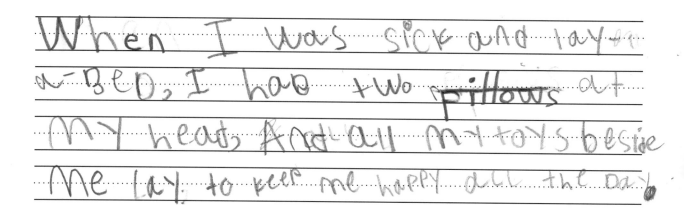

When I was sick and lay
a-Bed, I had two pillows at
my head, And all my toys beside
Me lay. to keep me happy all the Day

And sometimes for an hour or so
I watched my leaden soldiers go,
With different uniforms and drills,
Among the bed-clothes, through the hills.

And sometimes for an hour or so

And sometimes sent my ships in fleets
All up and down among the sheets;
Or brought my trees and houses out,
And planted cities all about.

And sometimes sent my ships in fleets

All up and down among the sheets

I was the giant great and still
That sits upon the pillow-hill,
And sees before him, dale and plain
The pleasant Land of Counterpane.

A GOOD PLAY

We built a ship upon the stairs
All made of the back-bedroom chairs,
And filled it full of sofa pillows
To go a-sailing on the billows.

We built a Ship upon the Stairs

We took a saw and several nails,
And water in the nursery pails;
And Tom said, "Let us also take
An apple and a slice of cake;"—
Which was enough for Tom and me
To go a-sailing on, till tea.

We sailed along for days and days,
And had the very best of plays;
But Tom fell out and hurt his knee,
So there was no one left but me.

MARCHING SONG

Bring the comb and play upon it!
   Marching, here we come!
Willie cocks his highland bonnet,
   Johnnie beats the drum.

Mary Jane commands the party,
    Peter leads the rear;
Feet in time, alert and hearty,
    Each a Grenadier!

All in the most martial manner
    Marching double-quick;
While the napkin like a banner
    Waves upon the stick!

Here's enough of fame and pillage,
Great commander Jane!
Now that we've been round the village,
Let's go home again.

THE HAYLOFT

Through all the pleasant meadow-side
    The grass grew shoulder-high,
Till the shining scythes went far and wide
    And cut it down to dry.

_____
. . . .
_____
_____
. . . .
_____
_____
. . . .
_____
_____
. . . .
_____

These green and sweetly smelling crops
    They led in wagons home;
And they piled them here in mountain-tops
    For mountaineers to roam.

_____
. . . .
_____
_____
. . . .
_____
_____
. . . .
_____
_____
. . . .
_____

Here is Mount Clear, Mount Rusty-Nail,
    Mount Eagle and Mount High;—
The mice that in these mountains dwell,
    No happier are than I!

O what a joy to clamber there,
    O what a place for play,
With the sweet, the dim, the dusty air,
    The happy hills of hay!

THE MOON

The moon has a face like the clock in the hall;
She shines on thieves on the garden wall,
On streets and fields and harbor quays,
And birdies asleep in the forks of the trees.

_____

The squalling cat and the squeaking mouse,
The howling dog by the door of the house,
The bat that lies in bed at noon,
All love to be out by the light of the moon.

But all of the things that belong to the day
Cuddle to sleep to be out of her way;
And flowers and children close their eyes
Till up in the morning the sun shall rise.

THE COW

The friendly cow all red and white,
    I love with all my heart:
She gives me cream with all her might,
    To eat with apple-tart.

_____

_____

_____

_____

_____

_____

She wanders lowing here and there,
    And yet she cannot stray,
All in the pleasant open air,
    The pleasant light of day.

And blown by all the winds that pass
    And wet with all the showers,
She walks among the meadow grass
    And eats the meadow flowers.

FOREIGN LANDS

Up into the cherry tree
Who should climb but little me?
I held the trunk with both my hands
And looked abroad on foreign lands.

Up into the Cherry tree
Who Should Climb but little me?

I saw the next door garden lie,
Adorned with flowers, before my eye,
And many pleasant places more
That I had never seen before.

I saw the dimpling river pass
And be the sky's blue looking-glass;
The dusty roads go up and down
With people tramping into town.

If I could find a higher tree
Farther and farther I should see,
To where the grown-up river slips
Into the sea among the ships.

To where the roads on either hand
Lead onward into fairy land,
Where all the children dine at five,
And all the playthings come alive.

SYSTEM

Every night my prayers I say,
And get my dinner every day;
And every day that I've been good
I get an orange after food.

_____
....
_____
....
_____
....
_____
....
_____
....
_____

The child that is not clean and neat,
With lots of toys and things to eat,
He is a naughty child, I'm sure—
Or else his dear papa is poor.

HAPPY THOUGHT

The world is so full of a number of things,
I'm sure we should all be as happy as kings

....

....

THE LAND OF NOD

From breakfast on through all the day
At home among my friends I stay,
But every night I go abroad
Afar into the Land of Nod.

_____
....
_____
_____
....
_____
_____
....
_____
_____
....
_____

All by myself I have to go,
With none to tell me what to do—
All alone beside the streams
And up the mountain-sides of dreams.

....

....

....

....

The strangest things are there for me,
Both things to eat and things to see,
And many frightening sights abroad
Till morning in the Land of Nod.

....

....

....

....

Try as I like to find the way,
I never can get back by day,
Nor can remember plain and clear
The curious music that I hear.

WINDY
NIGHTS

Whenever the moon and stars are set,
  Whenever the wind is high,
All night long in the dark and wet,
  A man goes riding by.
Late in the night when the fires are out,

....

....

....

....

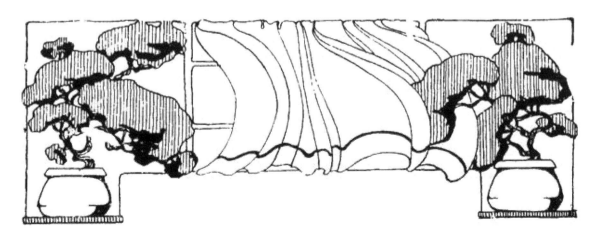

Why does he gallop and gallop about?
Whenever the trees are crying aloud,
    And ships are tossed at sea,
By, on the highway, low and loud,
    By at the gallop goes he.
By at the gallop he goes, and then
By he comes back at the gallop again.

TIME TO RISE

A birdie with a yellow bill
    Hopped up on the window sill,
Cocked his shining eye and said:
'Ain't you 'shamed, you sleepy-head?

A Birdie with a yellow Bill
hopped on the window sill
cocked his shining eye and said
Ain't You shamed you sleepy head?

✳ watch for upper and lower case letters
✳ watch for punctuation

39

FOREIGN CHILDREN

Little Indian, Sioux or Crow,
Little frosty Eskimo,
Little Turk or Japanee,
O! don't you wish that you were me?

Little Indian, Sioux or Crow,
Little frosty Eskimo,
Little Turk or Japanee,
O! don't you wish that you were me?

You have seen the scarlet trees
And the lions over seas;
You have eaten ostrich eggs,
And turned the turtles off their legs.

You seen the scarlet trees
And the lions over the seas;
You have eaten Ostrich eggs,
And turned the turtles Off their legs

Such a life is very fine,
But it's not so nice as mine:
You must often, as you trod,
Have wearied not to be abroad.

Such a life is very fine,
But it's not so nice as mine:
You must often, as you trod,
Have wearied not to be abroad.

You have curious things to eat,
I am fed on proper meat;
You must dwell beyond the foam,
But I am safe and live at home.

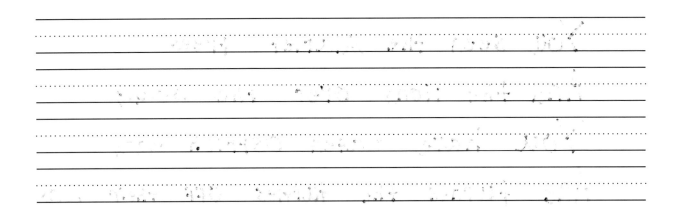

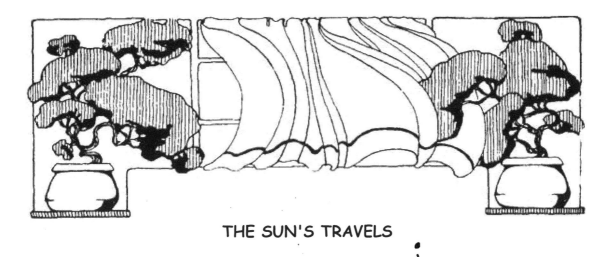

THE SUN'S TRAVELS

The sun is not a-bed when I
At night upon my pillow lie;
Still round the earth his way he takes,
And morning after morning makes.

the sun is not a-bed When I
At night upon my pillow lie;
still round the earth his way takes,
and morning After morning makes.

While here at home in shining day,
We round the sunny garden play,
Each little Indian sleepy-head
Is being kissed and put to bed.

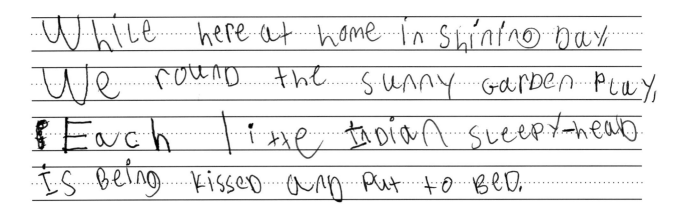

While here at home in shining day,
We round the sunny garden play,
Each little Indian sleepy-head
Is being kissed and put to bed.

And when at eve I rise from tea,
Day dawns beyond the Atlantic Sea;
And all the children in the West
Are getting up and being dressed.

And when at eve I rise from tea,
Day dawns beyond the Atlantic sea;

Singing

Of speckled eggs the birdie sings
    And nests among the trees;
The sailor sings of ropes and things
    In ships upon the seas.

Of speckeld eggs the birdie sings,

And nests among the trees;

The Sailor sings of ropes and things

In Ships upon the seas.

The children sing in far Japan,
    The children sing in Spain;
The organ with the organ man
    Is singing in the rain.

KEEPSAKE MILL

Over the borders, a sin without pardon,
    Breaking the branches and crawling below,
Out through the breach in the wall of the garden,
    Down by the banks of the river, we go.

Here is the mill with the humming of thunder,
    Here is the weir with the wonder of foam,
Here is the sluice with the race running under—
    Marvelous places, though handy to home!

Sounds of the village grow stiller and stiller,
    Stiller the note of the birds on the hill;
Dusty and dim are the eyes of the miller,
    Deaf are his ears with the moil of the mill.

Years may go by, and the wheel in the river
    Wheel as it wheels for us, children, to-day.
Wheel and keep roaring and foaming for ever
    Long after all of the boys are away.

Home from the Indies and home from the ocean,
    Heroes and soldiers we all shall come home;
Still we shall find the old mill wheel in motion,
    Turning and churning that river to foam.

You with the bean that I gave when we quarreled,
    I with your marble of Saturday last,
Honored and old and all gaily apparelled,
    Here we shall meet and remember the past.

THE UNSEEN PLAYMATE

When children are playing alone on the green,
In comes the playmate that never was seen.
When children are happy and lonely and good,
The Friend of the Children comes out of the wood.

When Children are Playing alone on the green,
In comes the Playmate that was never seen.
When Children are happy and lonely and good.
The friend of the Children comes out

Nobody heard him and nobody saw,
His is a picture you never could draw,
But he's sure to be present, abroad or at home,
When children are happy and playing alone.

Nobody heard him and no body saw,

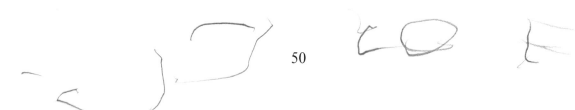

He lies in the laurels, he runs on the grass,
He sings when you tinkle the musical glass;
Whene'er you are happy and cannot tell why,
The Friend of the Children is sure to be by!

He loves to be little, he hates to be big,
'Tis he that inhabits the caves that you dig;
'Tis he when you play with your soldiers of tin
That sides with the Frenchman and never can win.

'Tis he, when at night you go off to your bed,
Bids you go to your sleep and not trouble your head;
For wherever they're lying, in cupboard or shelf,
'Tis he will take care of your playthings himself.

MY SHIP AND I.

O it's I that am the captain of a tidy little ship,
     Of a ship that goes a-sailing on the pond;
And my ship it keeps a-turning all around and all about;
But when I'm a little older, I shall find the secret out
     How to send my vessel sailing on beyond.

For I mean to grow as little as the dolly at the helm,
    And the dolly I intend to come alive;
And with him beside to help me, it's a-sailing I shall go,
It's a-sailing on the water, when the jolly breezes blow
And the vessel goes a divie-divie dive.

O it's then you'll see me sailing through the rushes and the reeds,
    And you'll hear the water singing at the prow;
For beside the dolly sailor, I'm to voyage and explore,
To land upon the island where no dolly was before,
    And to fire the penny cannon in the bow.

www.SheriGraham.com

Sheri Graham is a homeschool mom of 5 blessings. She enjoys being home with her family and using her talents to not only serve her family but to help others in their walks as wives and mothers (and daughters of the King!).

At the heart of Graham Family Ministries is ministering to the Christian family and using the gifts that the Lord has given each of us. Through our website (http://www.SheriGraham.com) we provide articles, downloads, ebooks, and links on homemaking and homeschooling topics, as well as information on other resources that hopefully will encourage you as you grow and learn together as a family. May the Lord bless each of you as you walk with Him each step of the way!

Be sure to subscribe to Sheri's blog to keep updated on new products, receive yummy recipes, and homemaking and homeschooling tips! You will be blessed!

You can find Sheri online at:
www.SheriGraham.com (My main website and blog)
www.SheriGraham.com/IntentionalPlanner (The Intentional Planner Website)
www.12weekholidayplanner.com (The Holiday Planner website)
www.Homeschooling-Central.com (My free homeschooling site!)

Warm-up

llllll llllll

OO O O oo O ooooooooooo

| | | | | | | | — — — — — —

૨ ᴐᴐᴐᴐᴄᴄ C

~~~~~~~~~~~~~

U U J C C C C C C C C 6
    ᴐ ᴐ ᴐ ᴐ ᴐ ᴐ

J J J ρ P

---

lines: | — | — | — | — | — | — | — | — | — | — |

C's: C C C C C C C C C

reverse ᴐ ᴐ ᴐᴐᴐᴐᴐᴐᴐᴐᴐ

Circles: O O O O O O O O O

tails: J 6 6 J 6 ᴐ

ᴐ ᴐ ᴐ ᴐ ᴐ

Made in the USA
Middletown, DE
02 November 2015